Bibliographic information published by the German National Library:

The German National Library lists this publication in the National Bibliography; detailed bibliographic data are available on the Internet at http://dnb.dnb.de .

Imprint:

Copyright © 2019 GRIN Verlag
Print and binding: Books on Demand GmbH, Norderstedt Germany
ISBN: 9783346052148

This book at GRIN:

https://www.grin.com/document/506345

Louie Sanlad

Parental involvement in learning. Implication to the academic achievement of learners

GRIN Verlag

GRIN - Your knowledge has value

Since its foundation in 1998, GRIN has specialized in publishing academic texts by students, college teachers and other academics as e-book and printed book. The website www.grin.com is an ideal platform for presenting term papers, final papers, scientific essays, dissertations and specialist books.

Visit us on the internet:

http://www.grin.com/

http://www.facebook.com/grincom

http://www.twitter.com/grin_com

Parental Involvement in Learning: Its Implication to the Academic Achievement of Learners

Dr.Louie G. Sanlad

Table of Content

ABSTRACT 2

INTRODUCTION 3

Parental Involvement 4

Parents as Stakeholders – Parents as Leaders 5

Parents as an Active Partner in Learning 5

Parent-School Connection 6

Challenges of Parental Involvement in Learning 6

Strategies for Encouraging Parental Involvement in Learning 6

Benefits of Parental Involvement 7

CONCLUSION 7

REFERENCES 9

1

ABSTRACT

The purpose of this paper is to discuss parental involvement in learning as to parents as active partner in learning, parent-school connection, parents as leaders, challenges of parental involvement in learning, strategies for encouraging parental involvement in learning, benefits of parental involvement and its implication to the academic achievement of learners. Parental involvement is a combination of commitment and active participation on the part of the parent to the school and to the student. There are many problems concerned with involvement. Organizations that advocate for education at the grassroots level are growing in number and they are working to organize parents, offering increased opportunities for parents to engage in education policy issues. This paper discussed parental involvement in learning, parents as leaders, parents as active partner in learning and parent-school connection. Also, it discussed the challenges of parental involvement in learning, strategies for encouraging parental involvement in learning and the benefits of parental involvement. After a thorough reviews of the previous studies and based on the readings, this paper concluded that parental involvement is associated with a wide range of positive child outcomes in schools, such as good academic skills, positive attitudes and social competence. This paper supports on researchers Kathleen Cotton and Karen Reed Wikelund (2001), "parental involvement in children's learning is positively related to achievement" for all types and ages of students and the more intense this involvement, the better the effects. The recommendation of this paper is to have a parental involvement in learning to make learning for children pleasant and encourages them to work even more as they seek to make those closest to them proud.

Keywords: academic achievement, education, parental involvement, school

INTRODUCTION

Education is a fundamental sector that every country needs to develop but government have limited resources. They face difficulties in providing quality education services that take into account, individual and community diversity. Parents' desire to measure teaching excellence is also compounded by their concern that excellent teaching is thereby reduced to a box-ticking exercise. The education institutions wishing to engage parents as a stakeholder group in a meaningful way is an inextricable part of society as well as the community to which it belongs. They are social subsystems which cannot function isolated from the hyper system of the social environment (Polydorou, 1995).

Moreover, productive collaborations demand that parents and teachers acknowledge the critical importance of each other's participation in the life of a child. This maturity of knowledge, understanding and empathy comes not only with a recognition of the child as the central purpose for the collaboration but also with a recognition of the need to maintain roles and relationships with children that are comprehensive, dynamic, and differentiated. Alone we can do so little; together we can do so much. There are many stakeholders in education each of whom needs to play his role effectively in order to help all our children learn better and reach their fullest potential. The pupils, parents, teachers, administrators, and community have the ultimate aim of helping all our children achieve the desired outcomes of education (Mortera, 2015).

When a community cares about its schools, schools perform better, and community support is a shared characteristic of high-performing schools. Many parents and guardians of K-12 students are already involved in basic activities like attending parent-teacher meetings and school events. A select group even go a step further by volunteering for class or school activities, or otherwise donating time and resources to their child's school—and with good reason. Such involvement is crucial because parent and community involvement correlate to higher academic progress and school improvement.

However, there are parents who do not engage with policy, yet often straightforward. They often have nothing to do with disinterest. Many parents find themselves stretched for time, energy, and resources. Moreover, advocacy calls for a specific set of civic skills, including a basic understanding of district and state education systems. For example, parents concerned about the underperformance of his child's school must first realize that most policy changes will occur at school level. They must learn when and where board meetings will occur, make arrangements to attend, and read and understand the policy matters that will be up for discussion—especially as it relates to their child's school. When this happens, several factors may be viewed as reasons: poor teaching-learning experience given by teachers, having incompetent faculty in the rosters of teachers, mismanaged school system by school heads, and poor leadership potential and misguided governance of the school administrator (Grauwe, 2004). All of this will go back to how the schools adopt and practically actualize the school-based management (Edge, 2000).

In the Philippines, to achieve the Education for All (EFA) objectives by 2015, the Department of Education is pursuing policy reforms under the Basic Education Sector Reform Agenda (BESRA). Key Reform Thrust 1 (KRT1) of BESRA is School-Based Management (SBM). SBM underscores the empowerment of key stakeholders in school communities to enable them to actively participate in the continuous improvement of schools towards the attainment of higher pupil/student learning outcomes (Abulencia, n.d.; Department of Education, 2006). In participatory democracy, 'other actors' are around the table. Parents desire a successful educational system for their children; while the students themselves want to receive good education. It's easy to imagine the influence the education system has on government officials, like city councilors and district representatives, as voters also base their decision on the way public officials show their support to the school system.

Specifically, the involvement and great partnership of pupils, parents, teachers, and community is very evident in the present situation of Mayor A.S. Fortuna Memorial Elementary, wherein the following projects were raised through the collaborative efforts of all, namely: The school pathway was cemented through the joint efforts of parents, and linkage with the City Personnel; the wash in school was finished and is now ready to use through the collaboration of parents; the ICT/e room window and roof (which secures the school's facilities) through the support of parents-teachers association; and lately school bags and supplies were given to the pupils by ABS-CBN Cebu Halad Kapamilya in collaboration of the parent volunteers. These endeavours meaningfully inspire and encourage the pupils to be in school. Volunteer reading partners come from all walks of life, some parents in the program volunteer to find themselves involved in education reform on the ground, providing mentorship and literacy intervention to students who need it most, changing the educational landscape in their communities.

Parental Involvement

Parental involvement refers to a situation where parents are directly involved in the education of their children, they involve themselves and are involved by the school and teachers in the learning process of their children, and they fulfill their duties as parents in making sure that the learner is assisted in the process of learning as much as they possibly can. It does not just refer to parents enquiring about the performance of a learner in schools, but also in them taking a role in communicating with their children with the aim of having a healthy relationship with them, so that the process of encouraging, mentoring, leading and inspiring may be genuine (Clinton & Hattie, 2013:324).

According to researchers Kathleen Cotton and Karen Reed Wikelund (2001), "parental involvement in children's learning is positively related to achievement" for all types and ages of students, and the more intense this involvement, the better the effects. There is an even greater effect for African-American students, a Duke University study claims. Joyce Epstein, the director of the Center on School, Family and Community Partnerships at Johns Hopkins University, identifies six types of parental involvement -- effective parenting, two-way communication with the school, volunteerism at the school, assisting with homework, participating in school governance and utilizing community resources.

According to Labahn (1995) parents are within their rights by insisting that children focus on their school work, because some children are lazy and come up with meaningless excuses in order to avoid doing their school work. Other benefits include those that are highlighted by Lemmer (2007:218) which include improved self-esteem, high rate of school attendance and positive social behaviour. Sivertsen (2015) adds that parental involvement is linked to improved behaviour, low levels of absenteeism and optimistic attitudes.

4

Parents as Stakeholders – Parents as Leaders

Parents make many decisions for families and children every day from what to eat for breakfast to structuring bedtime rituals and everything in-between. There are also the bigger decisions they are faced with such as finding a pediatrician, finding child care, and how best to support their children's learning in school to name a few. Having a child with special needs and/or health care needs exposes us to the disability world, to special education, to the medical world and possibly an entire host of governmental systems and agency programs we might have never realized existed before. They quickly become experts at finding resources and navigating systems. Such exposure can lead to involvement. Parents have a voice to share and an important story to tell. Their experiences are valuable and can be used to change and improve lives for the better. As such we are natural stakeholders for many different systems and programs and that can offer a path to become Parent Leaders.

Meaningful parent leadership occurs when parents gain the knowledge and skills to function in meaningful leadership roles and represent a 'parent voice' to help shape the direction of their families, programs and communities. Parent Leadership is successfully achieved when parents and professionals build effective partnerships and share responsibility, expertise and leadership in decisions being made that affect families and communities. The parents involved in these collaborations are called Parent Leaders.

Throughout the country, parents and professionals are working together in new ways. They are participating jointly in local, regional and national planning processes, collaborating as grant reviewers and program evaluators, and serving on advisory boards and coalitions. Working together, the voices of parents and professionals are shaping policy and practice to make a positive difference in the lives of children and families.

Parents as an Active Partner in Learning

Plan to have a family discussion each week. Try to pick a topic that emerges from your child's experiences at school. The more you familiarize yourself with the daily routines and activities at preschool, the more you'll be able to encourage this type of conversation. You can even extend the idea into an art project or create a family "book club" where everyone reads something relating to this theme.

Get the entire family involved. As often as possible, try to participate in field trips and classroom events such as potlucks, story parties, art shows, and class celebrations. Include grandparents, siblings, caregivers, and family friends. Your child will be delighted.

For parents and teachers alike, the goal is to play active roles in your child's life and to work towards forming a real bond. The child's best interest is always served when she has lots of people rooting for her and all the pieces of her life fit together. A strong home-school connection will set the stage for a child who will grow up with a love for learning.

Most educators believe in parent participation in children's education, but "participation" means different things to different teachers. To some, it might mean helping children with homework, returning notes and sending things in on time, and coming to a conference when notified to do so. But it should mean much more. Work with the teacher to find out some ways they can contribute to the classroom, but always be sure to do it within the guidelines they provide for them. By the same token, they have valuable insight about their child — no one knows her better than them — so it is important to take initiative and communicate that knowledge to the teacher throughout te school year.

Parent-School Connection

The connection parents have with their children's school is also important to academic success. The schools can support parents, such as outlining what's expected of parents, communicating with parents regarding what children are learning and providing an assortment of opportunities for parents to meet with school personnel. Through communication across home and school, parents and teachers can share information about children's progress. They can discuss their needs and interests to find the right opportunities to promote learning experiences. Meaningful conversation between parents and teachers creates mutual understanding. It also enhances both parents' and children's experiences with school.

Family-school relationships have been described as a safety net to promote children's learning and school experiences. Yet, parents differ in their skills, knowledge, resources and available time to support student engagement with school and learning. These differences are why cooperation and shared responsibility between parents and teachers are necessary to foster learning and students' success in school.

Challenges of Parental Involvement in Learning

According to Singh, Mbokodi and Msila (2004), one of the challenges that hampers effective parental involvement is **low income** that some receive per month, which leads them to working more jobs and not to spend enough time at home helping their children with their school work (Chavkin & William, 1989). The above causes a burden to the teachers because they are expected to produce good results yet they are no receiving any support from parents (Singh, Mbokodi & Msila, 2004). Another reason for parents not to be involved is the fact that schools sometimes **fail to create strong links between homes and schools** or an environment where parents do not feel welcomed in schools more especially low income earners. This situation is made worse by the fact that some parents are unable to read and write and they can only communicate in their mother tongue, which makes it difficult for them to assist their children with their homework (Lemmer, 2007).

Strategies for Encouraging Parental Involvement in Learning

There are varied strategies that the schools can use to get the parents involved in their children's learning. This could be done through **going out to the community**, or by encouraging parent participation by **publicizing through traditional means** (announcements, flyers) and non-traditional methods which include the **use of television, phone calls and sending emails**. The use of only traditional measures could tend to be ineffective in such cases where individual parents rely on non-traditional methods.

6

In a study conducted by Kwatubana and Makhalemele (2015), some schools did not use sound recruitment strategies that motivated parental involvement in school activities. In the same study schools in the Free State decided to use a raffle to select parents that were to be food handlers. This strategy can work well in situations where the school wants to eliminate discrimination by choosing individuals based on their status in the community or favouritism.

The use of effective strategies for encouraging parental involvement will enable the parents to be able to see the importance of being involved in their children's learning, and to be able to see the benefits that might result afterward. Also reaching families whose home language is not English by sending them information about their learners in their own home language in order to break the language barrier (Lemmer.2007).

Benefits of Parental Involvement

Parent-teacher partnership makes tremendous impact on children's education. According to Llamas and Tauzin (2016) parents become comfortable when the education system requires their involvement in school activities. The strong collaboration of parents with school authorities can lead to increased improvement in both physical and academic performance of the school. Hence, school administrators have to encourage parents to get involved and make contribution towards helping the school achieve its missions and goals (Sapungan & Sapungan, 2014).

Seeing parents involved in the education of their children is a good thing because it improves academic performance. Learners become more focused in their school work (Kwatubana & Makhalemele, 2015). This motivates learners not to give up easily when they do not understand a particular topic and will not bunk classes because they know that their parents are always monitoring their school attendance (Lemmer, 2007).

Learners, whose parents are involved, are active and ready to learn, they learn to be punctual from young age, they learn to be persistent as the parents would be continuously enquiring about their progress and they would not want to disappoint them. Through this parents can be able to make sure that their children succeed in school (Hornby & Lafaele, 2011).

CONCLUSION

After a thorough review of the previous studies and based on the readings, this paper concluded that parental involvement in learning makes the learner achiever. This can be achieved through parents' involvement in learning, to be an active partner in learning, and have parent-school connection. Hence, parental involvement is associated with a wide range of positive child outcomes in schools, such as good academic skills, positive attitudes and social competence. This paper supports on researchers Kathleen Cotton and Karen Reed Wikelund, "parental involvement in children's learning is positively related to achievement" for all types and ages of students and the more intense this involvement, the better the effects. This paper highly recommends to the school administrators as the implementer of the school policies to have a parental involvement in learning to make learning for children pleasant and encourage them to work even more as they seek to make those closest to them proud. This could be done through going out to the community, or by encouraging parent participation by publicizing through traditional means and non-traditional methods which include the use of television, phone calls and sending emails or posting in social media. Likewise, to make the parents motivitated to be involved in school, highlight the school achievements and present the performance indicators during the conduct of State of the School Address and give recognition to the active parents.

REFERENCES

Business Mirror (2018). Teachers need to build strong relationships with school stakeholders? Retrieved on July 12, 2019. <https://businessmirror.com.ph/2018/07/19/teachers-need-to-build-strong-relationships-with-school-stakeholders/>.

Cotton and Wikelund (2001). Date Retrieved on July 12, 2019. <https://living.thebump.com/parental-influence-student-education-7088.html>.

Engaging Stakeholders Including Parents and the Community to Sustain Improved Reading Outcomes? Retrieved on July 12, 2019. <https://www2.ed.gov/programs/readingfirst/support/stakeholderlores.pdf>.

Margaret Wood, Feng Su (2019). Parents as "stakeholders" and their conceptions of teaching excellence in English higher education. Retrieved on July 12, 2019. <https://www.emerald.com/insight/content/doi/10.1108/IJCED-05-2018-0010/full/html>.

Mortera (2015). Stakeholders Recognized as Partners in Progress. Retrieved on July 12, 2019. <https://www.depedmalaybalay.net/info/stakeholders-recognized-as-partners-in-progress.html>.

What can parents do to strengthen parent-school connections? Retrieved on July 12, 2019. <https://extension.umn.edu/parent-school-partnerships/what-can-parents-do-strengthen-parent-school-connections>.

Yit (2017). How parents and communities can influence and engage in education policy. https://readingpartners.org/blog/parents-engage-education-policy/.

YOUR KNOWLEDGE HAS VALUE

- We will publish your bachelor's and
  master's thesis, essays and papers

- Your own eBook and book -
  sold worldwide in all relevant shops

- Earn money with each sale

Upload your text at www.GRIN.com
and publish for free